CW00344318

SHIPWRECKS
of *the*
DORSET COAST

GORDON LE PARD

DORSET BOOKS

First published in Great Britain in 2005

Copyright © 2005 Gordon Le Pard

*All rights reserved. No part of this publication may be reproduced,
stored in a retrieval system, or transmitted in any form or by any means
without the prior permission of the copyright holder.*

British Library Cataloguing-in-Publication Data
A CIP record for this title is available from the British Library

ISBN 1 871164 48 6

DORSET BOOKS
*Dorset Books is a partnership between
Dorset County Council and Halsgrove*

Halsgrove House
Lower Moor Way
Tiverton, Devon EX16 6SS
Tel: 01884 243242
Fax: 01884 243325
email: sales@halsgrove.com
website: www.halsgrove.com

Printed and bound by The Cromwell Press, Trowbridge

About this Book

This is not a history of Dorset's shipwrecks, rather it is a collection of photographs of Dorset shipwrecks, and ships in trouble. Well known wrecks have been omitted if no suitable pictures were available, whilst little known incidents have been included if a good picture could be found.

Acknowledgements

I would like to thank Robin Ansell and the staff of Weymouth Reference Library, which supplied two thirds of the photographs in this book. Dave Stevens who supplied the bulk of the rest from his own collection of pictures of Dorset shipwrecks, and John Willows, an enthusiast for the works of Isambard Kingdom Brunel, for the remarkable picture of the *Great Eastern*.

Introduction

Sitting on the beach at Weymouth or Bournemouth on a summer's day, surrounded by holidaymakers, looking out over a calm sea dotted with gently bobbing yachts, it is difficult to think of the Dorset coast as being particularly dangerous to shipping. However, if you stand on Chesil Beach when a south-westerly gale rages, hearing the pebbles grind together under the pounding waves, then it is easy to appreciate the fear and respect with which this part of the coast was regarded by mariners.

As it is, the records speak for themselves, telling of over 2000 shipwrecks along the Dorset coast, and these are just the ones that have been written about. Before the middle of the nineteenth century it was only the notable shipwrecks, where a large vessel was lost, many people killed, or which were the subject of a court case, that were recorded. But even if a wreck was not considered worth recording, to the coastal population shipwrecks certainly had a value. The practice of *wrecking*, taking objects from wrecked ships, was commonplace. The legendary crime of wrecking, deliberately luring ships onto the coast, never took place in Dorset, indeed may never have taken place in Britain at all. Wrecks were regarded as part of the bounty of the sea, and a good year for wrecks would be regarded in the same light as a good year for mackerel. A local verse, almost a prayer, from the villages that lay behind Chesil Beach ran;

Blow wind, Rise storm,
Bring us a ship on shore before morn.

This was recorded as early as 1795, but the practise of wrecking was much older. In medieval times the 'Right of Wreck', the ownership of unclaimed shipwreck was a valuable right vested in local landowners. There were frequent disputes about these rights, indeed much of our knowledge of medieval shipwrecks comes from these disputes and the subsequent court cases. In 1275 the town of Bridport was trying to take control of Bridport harbour (now West Bay). In their submission to the king they claimed that;

> The Abbot of Cernel [Cerne Abbas] and the Prior of Frompton [Frampton] take all wreck coming from the sea between two cliffs on each side of the weir belonging to the Borough of Bridport, by what authority they know not.

Five years later the Abbot of Cerne brought a case against sixteen men of Bridport for;

> Taking by force of arms and ill treatment certain goods and chattels which were wreck of the sea within his manor. viz., ship's woodwork, planks and ironwork of wrecks.

The men charged were leading citizens of the town, and included five who had served as bailiffs and one major ship owner.

By the eighteenth century the rights of wreck claimed by local landowners had been strictly curtailed to respect the rights of the original owner. However, the bulk of the population had a simpler view: as far as they were concerned all shipwrecks were fair game.

In 1749 the Dutch ship *De Hoop* (generally anglicized as *The Hope*) was driven onto Chesil Beach opposite the village of Fleet. The crew managed to make their way to safety, then the local villagers learnt there was gold on board. The news spread like wildfire and within days a crowd of ten thousand people were on the beach searching for treasure. They were only dispersed, and sent back to their homes, by mounted troops. The authorities arrested several men for stealing gold from the wreck, but when the first of them was brought to trial, he was acquitted! The evidence had been overwhelming but, as one commenter said at the time, it would have been difficult to have chosen a jury in Dorset that year, which did not include someone who had been on the beach searching for gold!

Fifty years later, in 1795, when several troop ships were wrecked on Chesil Beach, the wrecking reached new levels of horror. One survivor staggered up the Beach:

Weakened as he was, and encumbered with his wet clothes, he got on the other side of the stony bank, and … looking around him over the dreary beach, his first idea was, that he was thrown on an uninhabited coast. At length he saw a fishing boat, and approaching it, heard the groans of a Veteran of the 63rd regiment, who had his leg dreadfully fractured, whom he attempted to relieve. But he could do nothing alone, … at length he perceived a man at some distance, to whom he hastened, and enquired eagerly if a Surgeon could be procured for a poor creature with a broken limb, who lay under the boat.

The man probably shewed no great alacrity, for Master Smith found it necessary to purchase his good offices by giving him half a guinea, which he imagined would engage him to seek for a surgeon. The man Pocketed the half guinea with the greatest composure, then, saying he was a King's Officer, and must see what bales of goods were driven on shore, he hastened away without giving himself any farther trouble, than telling Master Smith that there was a ferry about four miles off, by which he might get to Weymouth.

(Charlotte Smith, *Narrative of the Loss of* The Catharine, Venus, *and* Piedmont *etc.*)

The law was very strict on wrecking, but it was difficult to enforce. Not only could the jury be sympathetic to the wrecker, but the officials who were supposed to prevent wrecking were few, and were easily intimidated. So other means were tried to make the people change their ways. Thomas Francklyn, Rector of Langton Herring and Vicar of Fleet wrote a sermon entitled *Serious Advice and Fair Warning To all that live upon the Sea-Coast of England and Wales, Particularly To those in the neighbourhood of Weymouth and Portland* which emphasised how evil wrecking was, and what a great sin it was to steal from a shipwreck. This was first preached in the tiny church at Chickerell on 22 December 1753. A more recent Vicar of Chickerell tried, as an experiment, to preach the sermon (to an empty church) to see how long it would take – it took him nearly two hours! Sermons of this type, and probably this length, were preached annually at many churches around the coast of England, though their effect was limited. Wrecking continued to be a major problem along the Dorset coast until well into the nineteenth century, indeed even today some people believe that if they find an object from a wrecked ship it is automatically theirs – it isn't and the penalties for taking it are still severe.

It will have been noticed that many of the wrecks mentioned took place along Chesil Beach. This is not a coincidence. Chesil Beach, and the Island of Portland, which the Beach links to the mainland, is the worst place in Dorset, and one of the worst places in Britain, for shipwrecks. The long curved western edge of Lyme Bay, formed by Chesil Beach, ends at Portland which hangs like a hook into the English Channel waiting to catch mariners. An American author has coined a name for a feature like this, a *Ship Trap*. The prevailing wind is south westerly, blowing straight onto Chesil Beach and the western side of Portland, creating a classic lee shore. The sea bed of Lyme Bay provided poor holding for anchors, so there was little hope for a sailing vessel to anchor and ride out a south-westerly gale. All the captain could do, if he was unable to sail round Portland Bill to safety, was beat up and down off Chesil Beach, gradually getting closer, and praying that the wind would drop before his vessel was driven ashore. If this happened he had two terrible alternatives. The west coast of Portland has sheer cliffs dropping into the sea, with broken rocks at the base. Further west Chesil Beach looks a better choice, but can be even worse. A steep shingle beach that drops precipitously into the sea:

And once on the beach, the sea has little mercy, for the water is deep right in, and the waves curl over full on the pebbles with a weight no timbers can withstand. Then if the poor fellows try to save themselves, there is a deadly undertow or rush-back of the water, which sucks them off their legs, and carries them again under the thundering waves. It is that back-suck of the pebbles that you may hear for miles inland, even at Dorchester, on still nights long after the winds that caused it have sunk, and which makes people turn in their beds, and thank God they are not fighting with the sea on Moonfleet [Chesil] Beach.

(J. Meade Faulkner, *Moonfleet*.)

If a sailing ship was being driven onto Chesil Beach there was one, very desperate, measure the captain could take to save the crew. To order the men to set what sail they could – and steer straight for the Beach. If they were lucky the masts would collapse and form a bridge between the wreck and shore, down which the men could scramble to safety. As the Norwegian barque *Patria* was being driven towards the shore, during an October gale in 1903:

The skipper called us aft.

'Boys,' he said, 'we have the choice between Chesil Bank and the cliffs of Portland. I think there is a chance of saving some of you if I attempt to sail her up on the beach instead of drifting in. Any objections?'

Chips spoke up for all of us: 'No sir, sail her up. It's the only way.'

'Square away fore and mainyards!' came the order 'Up helm!'

We jumped to it with a curious feeling of relief. The tension and weary waiting was over and we were facing a straight issue. 'Shake out the reef in the main upper topsail' came the next order and we youngsters swarmed up to cast off the reef points. 'Sea boots off and every man for himself!'

(A.H. Rasmussen, *Sea Fever.*)

By good fortune a crowd had gathered to see another vessel which had been wrecked the previous day on Chesil Beach and there were plenty of helpers to assist in the rescue. All the crew of the *Patria* were saved, though one man lost a leg and another went mad. Seventy-five years earlier, in 1824, the sloop *Ebenezer* was even more fortunate. During one of the worst storms ever to hit the Dorset coast:

An ordnance sloop laden with stores was being driven by the gale towards the fatal beach, when an enormous wave seized hold of the ship, lifted it up, and carried it to the very top of the bank, where it was left, to its astonishment, high and dry. The sailors, who had all hope battered out of them, stepped over the bulwarks on to the beach, and walked, wet and amazed, into Portland, where they were greeted by some as liars, by others as men who had come out of the jaws of death. As they crawled into the first tavern in the town, and, above the howling of the wind and the rattling of casements, told how their sloop had been lifted by the sea out of the West Bay and deposited unhurt on the top of Chesil Beach, the men in jerseys who were sheltering round the fire must have stared at them open-mouthed. The doubters were perforce convinced when in the course of days the sloop was launched down the far bank into the Fleet, and was brought round to Weymouth Bay by this unfamiliar overland route. The sloop was a craft of ninety-five tons, by name the "Ebenezer," and in the fearsome voyage only two on board were drowned.

(Sir Frederick Treves *Highways and Byways in Dorset.*)

This storm, in 1824, marked the beginning of a new attitude to wrecks. Whilst there had always been cases of individual heroism, where local men risked their lives trying to save people from shipwreck, these had been few and far between compared with the almost universal practice of wrecking. However times were changing and a committee had just been formed in London, with the title of 'The National Society for the Preservation of Lives from Shipwreck.' This was trying to encourage people around the coast to set up local life saving organisations. In Dorset the Vicar of Abbotsbury, the Reverend Mr Murray took up the challenge. He had been badly affected by the great storm, leading parties along the beach picking up the bodies of drowned sailors; in all he had buried eighteen victims of the storm. He suffered greatly as a result – today we would talk about post-traumatic stress – and became obsessed with the idea that such a disaster should not be allowed to happen again. He was the ideal leader of a campaign to establish a local committee of the Society. He was very successful in raising public support, and within months rescue equipment was being provided along the coast. The National Society for the Preservation of Lives from Shipwreck became, in due course, the Royal National Lifeboat Institution. The courage and dedication of the lifeboat crews is legendary, summed up by an epitaph on the grave of a former coxswain of the Poole lifeboat – *Lifeboatmen never turn back.*

The Pictures

There has long been a fascination with shipwrecks; people have been thrilled with stories and pictures of shipwreck from the earliest times. One need only think of the tale of St Paul, shipwrecked on the coast of Malta. As soon as cameras had been invented, they were being used to record shipwrecks, the earliest photograph in this book dates from 1859 and shows the *Great Eastern* being repaired in Portland Harbour following an explosion. A shipwreck was an exciting event and photographs show this, for example a family group posing in front of the *Dorothea* on Chesil Beach. Wrecks such as the *Alioth* at West Bay and the *Madeleine Tristan* at Chesil Cove were popular tourist attractions; pictures show the crowds gathered to see the wreck and there are people still alive today who can remember being taken to see the shipwreck as a Sunday afternoon treat!

The photographs in this book come from a variety of sources, some were taken by individuals as their own record of an unusual occurrence, however many were originally produced as postcards. Newspapers had few, if any, illustrations and a postcard provided a visual record of an important event. Postcards were produced on a variety of subjects, public events, notable weddings and funerals, disasters such as fires, floods and, of course, shipwrecks.

Great Eastern

This picture is probably the earliest photograph of a ship in difficulty off the Dorset coast, indeed it may be the earliest photograph of a ship in these waters. Taken in September 1859, it shows the *Great Eastern*, the third, final and greatest ship built by the great Victorian engineer, Isambard Kingdom Brunel.

On 7 September the *Great Eastern* was proceeding down channel at the start of her maiden voyage. Off Hastings the water jacket round Number 1 funnel exploded, killing several men. Despite the damage the ship continued to Portland where she arrived on 10 September, and moored in the partly completed Portland Harbour. Here she was repaired, her damaged funnel was removed and a new one built, incorporating several design changes to ensure the accident didn't happen again.

While she lay in the harbour the *Great Eastern* became a tourist attraction. The Victorian public loved innovative engineering projects and contemporary illustrations often show family parties wandering around industrial complexes. Over six thousand people paid half a crown (12½ p) to visit the ship and watch the repair work. The stereo photograph was taken at this time.

Opposite: *The* Great Eastern *under repair in Portland Harbour, September 1859. The absence of Number 1 funnel proves that this picture must date from this time.*

Premier

The *Premier* was a very old ship, approaching the end of her career, when she was in collision with HM Submarine *Rainbow*.

The *Premier* had arrived in Weymouth in 1859, in order to cope with the expected increase in tourists wishing to see the *Great Eastern* on her planned stop in Portland Harbour during her maiden voyage. She continued in service with Cosens, the famous Weymouth paddle steamer company, for the next six decades, taking tourists from Weymouth to Portland, Lulworth Cove and other places of interest.

On the morning of the 28 June 1932 she was taking 150 passengers to Portland. Her course lay along the outside of Portland Breakwater; at the same time HMS *Rainbow* was leaving the harbour. The two vessels didn't see each other until it was too late. *Rainbow* struck the *Premier* close to her bow. This was fortunate as this was just in front of her only watertight bulkhead, which probably prevented a tragedy. As it was her passengers only suffered minor bruises, and all returned safely to Weymouth in the damaged paddle steamer under her own power.

The *Premier* was rapidly repaired and was back in service in little more than two weeks.

The bow of HMS Rainbow *showing the damage caused when she struck PS* Premier.

Clockwise, starting
top right:

The damaged side of
PS Premier.

In happier days, the Premier
steams past the 'big boats'
in Weymouth Bay.

PS Premier *on her way to*
the breakers yard, passing
through Town Bridge,
Weymouth in April 1938.

Shamrock III

At the beginning of the twentieth century the waters of Weymouth Bay were frequently the venue for major yacht races. Llewellyn Pridham described these events in *The Dorset Coastline*:

'What more glorious spectacle can be imagined than these yachts – *the big boats* – which used to compete in the Royal Dorset Yacht Club's regatta. To be afloat when these craft were racing was an experience never to be forgotten: canvases aglow with the yellow sunlight shining through the taut panels: driving past with an organ note of drumming sails; spray at their bows, the green water sliding away under the counter, going … "at a speed of knots!"'

But sometimes these spectacular craft came to grief. This photograph shows *Shamrock III* after being dismasted on 17 April 1903. The elegant steam yacht in the background may be that owned by Sir Thomas Lipton, the owner of *Shamrock III*.

La Servannaise

In 1924 Weymouth lifeboat station received its first motor lifeboat, the *Samuel Oakes*. It was not long before she made her first rescue. The French brigantine, *La Servannaise* had been anchored off Redcliff Point on New Years Day 1925, when a strong south-westerly gale had driven her across the bows of the oil tanker *British Lady*. Their anchor chains had become locked together and she smashed into the side of the steamer. Her bowsprit was carried away and she was partially dismasted. The *Samuel Oakes* stood by as the two vessels were separated, and remained on station as *La Servannaise* was towed into Weymouth on the morning of 3 January 1925.

Arguenon

On Christmas morning 1930 people in Weymouth awoke to find the French yacht *Arguenon* on the sands. She had dragged her anchor in the bay, and drifted ashore during the night. Much to the delight of local children she remained there for several weeks until she was floated off at the next spring tide, an event which made for a very memorable Christmas holiday.

Stuart

The *Stuart* was at anchor in Portland Harbour on the night of 13 February 1899, when a severe westerly gale struck. Her anchor started dragging and her captain, realising she was endangering other vessels in the anchorage, slipped her cable and let her drift. The wind pushed her across the harbour, the crew of the *Stuart* desperately using whatever means they could to steer her away from other vessels.

The northern breakwater was still under construction, and part was covered at high water. Bumping hard the *Stuart* slid over the breakwater into deeper water. At this point, understandably, the crew decided to leave the vessel and let her drift across Weymouth Bay.

She finally ran aground on Preston Beach. Salvage proved easy as she was a new, well built vessel. At the next spring tide she was towed off and returned to Portland Harbour under her own steam.

Minx

The *Minx* was a steam powered coal barge, which had broken free from her moorings in Portland Harbour in November 1927. With no crew on board she drifted across Weymouth Bay and ran onto the rocks at Osmington Mills. Salvage was attempted but was rapidly given up. Subsequently the local people 'salvaged' a considerable amount of coal, and local tradition says that the cottages in Osmington Mills were very warm and cosy that Christmas!

The Minx *off Osmington Mills. Her remains still project above water today.*

Francis

The yacht *Francis* broke free from her mooring in Weymouth Bay and drifted ashore on 5 July 1933. Whilst waiting for a suitable tide to float her off, she became an instant, and very popular, tourist attraction.

Ardente

It is very rare for a lifeboat to be photographed carrying out a rescue, the conditions being, understandably, usually against it. This makes this picture of the Weymouth rowing lifeboat *Friern Watch* rescuing the crew of the French schooner *Ardente* particularly interesting. On 11 December 1914 the *Ardente* was moored in Weymouth Bay. As the wind rose her anchor dragged and she was driven towards Preston Beach. The *Friern Watch* tried to get a line onboard so a tug could tow her to safety, but this proved impossible. The lifeboat crew then rowed close into the French vessel and managed to get the five crew members off just before she struck.

Opposite: *The* Friern Watch *approaching the* Ardente. *Her crew can be seen on the ships side awaiting rescue.*

Right: *The* Ardente *on Preston Beach after the rescue of the crew. She was later salvaged.*

Warspite's drifter

This is another rare photograph of a rescue taking place. The story of the rescue is told in detail by Graham Farr in *Wreck and Rescue on the Dorset Coast*.

'On October 5th 1920, the lifeboat carried out a difficult service … The drifter attached to HMS *Warspite* for stores, personnel and ammunition duties, stranded on the Mixen Reef in rough seas whipped up by a strong south-easterly breeze. The *Charles Deere James*, a reserve lifeboat temporarily on the station, was asked to stand by. She remained at hand in very unpleasant conditions until a tug got a hawser to the drifter and when she was refloated in a leaking state accompanied her into harbour in case she should suddenly founder.'

Amy

The *Amy* is an unusual wreck. A small schooner, she was sunk deliberately on 15 March 1928 to provide suitably spectacular special effects for the film 'Q Ships'. This film, which starred Val Gielgud, brother of Sir John Gielgud, told, in a rather over dramatised manner, the story of the Q Ships.

These were small warships disguised as merchantmen, which went hunting for U Boats. At this time, during the First World War, U Boats often surfaced beside merchantmen and either sank them by gunfire or placed explosives on board. The Q Ship would wait until the U Boat was close then run up the White Ensign, and attack. This was very dangerous as the U Boats were often suspicious and attacked the Q Ship from a distance. Sometime the crews would remain hidden and wait while their ship was destroyed around them just for a chance to sink the U Boat.

In the English Channel, off the Dorset coast, lie the remains of two U Boats, *UB19* and *UC18*, both victims of Q Ships.

Right: Amy *leaving Weymouth on her final voyage.*

Below: Amy *blown up, the 'dazzle' camouflage on her port side clearly seen. Her starboard side was left plain, as can be seen on the preceding picture. This was so her sinking could be filmed from both sides so she could play the role of two U Boat victims in the film.*

British Inventor

The tanker *British Inventor* struck a mine whilst in convoy 5 miles off St Aldhelm's Head on 13 June 1940. She broke in two, the fore part sinking on the Lulworth Banks, whilst the stern section was towed into Portland Harbour. A month later this section was towed to Southampton, sold as scrap and broken up.

Left: *In a sinking condition in Portland Harbour.*

Opposite: *Refloated so she could be towed to the breakers yard.*

L 24

The *L24* had been completed in 1919, too late to see action in the First World War. As a result she was used for training crews of submariners, and on training exercises with other naval vessels. It was on one of these that she met her end. In January 1924 she was she was carrying out dummy attack runs on a group of warships. At 11.13 on the 10th men on board the battleship HMS *Resolution* felt a slight jolt and those on watch saw a disturbance in the water. Later that day it was realised that the *L24* had been sunk. The submarine was located the following day, using what was described by the press as a 'secret ray' that could detect metal, clearly an early type of magnetometer (these are still used to locate wrecks today). Sadly bad weather prevented divers reaching the wreck for several days. There were no survivors, though there were signs that some of the crew had tried to escape, but in the freezing water they had no chance.

Memorial cards were often produced after submarine disasters, with pictures of the vessel and members of the crew.

M2

The submarine *M2* is one of the most famous wrecks in Dorset waters. She was the world's first fully functional aircraft-carrying submarine. The idea of combining submarines and aircraft had been raised during the First World War, but not with any success. Various countries tried during the years after the war, notably America, France, Japan and Great Britain.

The *M2* had originally been built with a massive 12 inch gun, but this was removed as a result of an international disarmament treaty. The large submarine became a test bed, and was fitted with a watertight aircraft hangar and catapult launch ramp. During operations the aircrew entered the hangar from the submarine, whilst she was still submerged. As soon as she surfaced the hangar doors were opened and the aircraft run out onto the launching ramp. The wings were folded out and the aircraft launched. After carrying out its mission the float plane would land beside the *M2* to be picked up.

On 26 January 1932 she was carrying out exercises off Portland. She dived at about 10.30 am and was never heard of again. By the afternoon she was reported as missing and the search started, using pioneering echo sounding gear. They searched the area but didn't locate the wreck until 2 February. By this time there was no hope of anybody being alive, but work began at once on trying to salvage the wreck as well as finding out what went wrong.

After investigation it was decided that the most likely cause of the disaster was that the hangar doors had been opened before the hatch linking the hangar and the submarine had been closed, water flooded in and the *M2* sank.

After nearly a year of salvage operations the submarine was abandoned and she still lies on seabed in Lyme Bay. The Royal Navy then gave up the idea of an aircraft-carrying submarine, as did the Americans. However, the Japanese continued with their experiments and massive submarine aircraft carriers operated with some success during the Second World War. Other navies were also interested in the *M2*, the press reports of the search and salvage operations giving the German Navy the first clues that the British had developed ASDIC.

Left: *Over the wreck of the M2 the bubbles show where air is being pumped into the submarine in the attempt to raise it.*

Below: *Salvage work on M2 in West Bay shows HMS Tedworth and salvage vessels.*

Opposite: *Memorial card for the M2 disaster.*

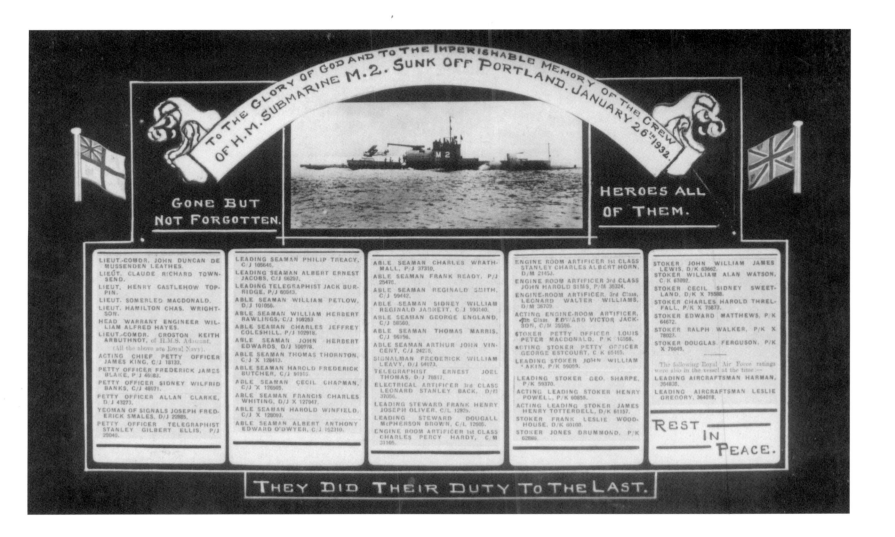

Cerera

The *Cerera* was a Russian cargo ship bound for Odessa. Poor visibility led to her running aground on the ledges just to the east of St Aldhelm's Head. Tugs got her off successfully and she was towed into Portland Harbour for repairs. Some early accounts name this vessel as the *Hepepa*. This was an anglicised version of the Cyrillic letters that spelt out her name.

Left: *The* Cerera *aground under St Aldhelm's Head.*

Opposite: *The* Cerera *and a salvage vessel in Portland Harbour.*

Montanes

The story of the wrecking of the *Montanes* is one of confusion and mistaken messages, but happily with no serious consequences.

Bound from Seville with a very mixed cargo of silver and manganese ores, wine and oranges the *Montanes* was making for Portland to take on fuel. In dense fog her lookout failed to see the Shambles Lightship to the south of Portland Bill, so she continued sailing north-eastwards until she ran onto the rocks directly under St Aldhelm's Head. Her captain sent up flares which were seen by the coastguard who contacted the Swanage lifeboat, but the message was not clearly relayed and the boat wasn't launched. Instead the message was passed onto Poole which immediately launched their lifeboat.

Meanwhile two of the coastguards had launched their own boat and taken off the crew of the *Montanes*, landing the men safely in Chapman's Pool. Realising that the Poole lifeboat was on its way a message was sent ordering its return. The crew of the Poole lifeboat were much praised for the quick and efficient way in which they had launched their lifeboat and got it underway.

Treveal

The tale of the wreck of the *Treveal* is one of the saddest tales of shipwreck along the Dorset Coast.

The *Treveal* was homeward bound from Calcutta with a cargo of jute and manganese ore. On 19 January 1920 she arrived in Weymouth Bay expecting to pick up a pilot. Unfortunately none was available and she was ordered to continue. At this point things began to go wrong. A basic navigational error led to her running onto the Kimmeridge Ledges below St Aldhelm's Head. At first there was little concern, the ship seemed undamaged and weather was fair. A tug was ordered and, after a little delay, as the crew needed to be assembled, it set out from Portland Harbour.

During the night the weather worsened and the tug failed to find the ship. On returning to harbour the tugs crew learnt that the *Treveal* was in serious difficulties so they returned to the wreck. This time they found the *Treveal* but the weather was now so bad that the tug was unable to get close to the wreck. The lifeboat was on its way, but the crew of the *Treveal* didn't know this and took to their own boats. Trying to make a landing in Chapman's Pool the boats were swamped. Of the 43 crew, only seven survived.

Two days later, when the storm was over, a local boatman and his daughter went out to the wreck to see if the animals, which they had learnt were on board, were still alive. They discovered that the captain's cabin was dry and the stove still slightly warm. If the crew had remained on board, they would all have lived.

Above: *The* Treveal *broken in two on the Kimmeridge Ledges.*

Right: *Coming to look at the wreck.*

Sand Dart

On March 10th 1962, there was a casualty which turned into a long drawn salvage operation. Soon after three in the morning the coastguard on top of St Alban's [Aldhelm's] Head realised that a vessel had gone ashore almost exactly below his lookout. He could not see her as there was fog and drizzling rain, but he at once informed the lifeboat. The lifeboat was launched into a moderate sea and found the motor sand dredger *Sand Dart* on the rocks, bumping heavily with the swell. Five of the crew were taken off at the master's request, but he stayed aboard with the mate and engineer to do what was possible towards salvage.

Salvage prospects looked grim, but some rocks were blasted away, motors were put aboard to pump and all accessible leaks stopped. However there was no success on the next high tides in April and then gales blew up which drove her farther inshore. Early on the morning of May 25th, when there was nobody on board, fire broke out. By a happy mischance a signal rocket was ignited and this warned the Coastguard. Firemen were brought quickly to the scene as the salvors had left gelignite on board to blast rocks, but fortunately this was saved before the fire got near. They extinguished the fire in a few hours after the bridge and accommodation were completely gutted.

It now looked a hopeless case for salvage but the little ship was strongly built, and the salvors were not the sort to give up easily. They finally refloated her on October 14th, and towed her to Portland to be beached and patched.

Wreck and Rescue on the Dorset Coast.

Hood

HMS *Hood* was a 380-foot-long, 14000-ton battleship built in 1891 at the height of the *Pax Britannica*. During her career she never fired a shot in anger, but instead was employed on the Mediterranean station where she 'showed the flag' to good effect for nine years. Her heavy armour and low freeboard combined to make her sail very poorly; however, she looked impressive and was ideal for the role in which she was placed.

By 1914 she was obsolete and was considered only fit for the scrapyard, but then it was realised that the southern entrance to Portland Harbour was very susceptible to an attack by submarines and torpedoes. It was decided to block the entrance, and HMS *Hood* was used to the purpose. Towed out to the entrance in November 1914 she was scuttled there. It was intended to sink her vertically, but she turned turtle as she sank.

She still lies across the entrance, and is ironically one of the best preserved battleships of her period in existence.

Left: *The* Hood *in position.*

The Hood *sinking.*

Robert J. (George) Symonds was a diver in Portland Harbour who is known as the, 'man who sank the *Hood*'. It was intended to sink the *Hood* by opening her sea-cocks. However, she didn't sink fast enough, and began to drift out of position, so George Symonds was sent down to place explosives on the hull. This blew a hole in her hull and sank her exactly across the harbour entrance.

George Symonds is the diver on the left.

Persian Monarch

In foggy conditions, on the night of 29 October 1886, the *Persian Monarch*, a 3900-ton steamer, ran straight onto Portland Breakwater under full power. Remarkably she suffered little damage and was easily towed off two weeks later. Much more difficult had been the salvage of her cargo, of live cattle!

Dinnington

On 21 March 1901 the *Dinnington* was trying to enter Portland Harbour in a gale. The crew failed to see the warning light and she ran straight onto the Northern Breakwater, then under construction. The crew were all rescued and, surprisingly enough, so was the *Dinnington*. She was re-floated several weeks later with remarkably little damage.

Devonia

The *Devonia* was another casualty of the Portland Breakwater. On 13 September 1912 her anchor slipped in bad weather and she was blown, bow first onto the breakwater. She suffered no damage and was able to restart her engines, to assist in the salvage operation, when she was eventually refloated shortly afterwards.

Opposite: *Towing the* Devonia *off the breakwater.*

Freewill

In December 1922 the oil tanker *Scandinavia* struck the Portland Breakwater during a blizzard, several plates were knocked out of her bottom and she swiftly sank. The wreck was sold for breaking up to the firm of Turners of Weymouth.

Work started on dismantling the *Scandinavia* early in 1923, and on 3 April the tug *Freewill* was at work on the site. She was trying to lift a piece of iron plate when her bow hawser snapped. She swung over the part of the breakwater which had sunk the *Scandinavia* – there was a heavy swell that day which dropped her down heavily on the rocks. She began to leak and sank alongside the vessel she had come to salvage. Later that year, after salvage work on the *Scandinavia* had been completed, the remains of the *Freewill* were salvaged in their turn.

Crown of Denmark

The two-masted sailing barge *Crown of Denmark* slipped its anchor in a strong south-westerly wind on 13 January 1931. She was swept across Portland Harbour and struck the breakwater. As waves pounded on the vessel, her crew managed to make their way onto the breakwater where they then spent several uncomfortable hours before they were rescued. Despite her perilous position she was refloated successfully in February and towed across the harbour to be beached at Castletown for repairs.

Curiously the following year Captain Howard of the *Crown of Denmark* was one of the witnesses to the sinking of the *M2* submarine.

Deveron

Early in the morning on 19 June 1905, the schooner *Deveron* was at anchor in Portland Harbour. A teenage boy was the only sailor on deck. As he was watching a squadron of destroyers leaving the harbour in line astern, the last ship in line, HMS *Conflict* turned wide and struck the *Deveron*, then continued on her way without waiting to see what happened to the ship she had struck. The schooner sank within minutes, but happily the crew all got off in time. Several weeks later she was raised successfully. The officer on watch on the *Conflict* was severely reprimanded.

Haytian

The *Haytian* was both a lucky, and unlucky ship. Unlucky because she sank on three occasions, and lucky because she was raised twice and no one was hurt on any of her sinkings.

She had been originally built as a luxury liner for the West Indian run in 1875, but by 1910 she had declined in importance and was being used as a coal hulk in Portland Harbour.

Early on the morning of 18 July 1910 the cargo ship *Nymphaea* approached the *Haytian* to take on coal. Two things then went wrong, her engine jammed and could not be put into reverse, and then her anchor cable stuck. Unable to stop, the *Nymphaea* hit the *Haytian* amidships. She rapidly took on water and sank two hours later. The crews of the tugs that had gathered to try and tow the *Haytian* into shallow water, were horrified to see hundreds of rats pour out of her as she settled in the water, 'like those which followed the Pied Piper of Hamelin', as one newspaper reported.

Opposite: The Haytian *sunk in 1910.*

A few weeks later the *Haytian* was raised and continued as a coal hulk for nearly thirty years, until 18 February 1937 when she was rammed by HMS *PC74* and sunk for the second time. This time she was raised several months later by a local salvage expert, George Louis Basso. Fortunately a member of his team took a series of photographs showing the raising of the *Haytian*.

The *Haytian* remained in the Harbour for a few more years, before finally being scuttled for the third and final time.

The damage caused to HMS PC74.

The Haytian *sunk in 1937 – only the masts showing.*

The salvage vessel Recovery *of Leith.*

Pumping out the coffer dams.

After only a one hour's pumping, she was out of the water.

By the following day she had steam in her boiler.

Himalaya

The *Himalaya* was an old ship – a veteran of the Crimean War – which sank in the Second World War.

She had been intended for the P&O shipping company when she was laid down in 1852 as a three-masted, ocean-going, paddle steamer. However, whilst she was being built, the *Great Britain*, the first ocean-going iron screw ship, proved that the future lay with screw propulsion. So the *Himalaya*'s design was altered to take a screw, and she became the second great iron screw ship: indeed when she was built she was the largest ship in the world.

Shortly after completion she was hired by the Admiralty for use as a troopship, carrying men, horses and supplies out to the Crimean War, where she was very popular with the soldiers because of the quality of the accommodation she provided. As a result she was bought by the government and continued to be used as a troopship until 1895. Then she was converted to a coal hulk and moved to Portland Harbour.

On 12 June 1940 a JU88 dropped four bombs on her, one exploding and sending her to the bottom. The Germans were so impressed by her size they claimed to have sunk a battleship!

The photograph shows her as a coal hulk moored in Portland Harbour, her elegant curved stern the only evidence of her former grandeur.

Angela

The *Angela* was a very lucky vessel. On 26 May 1907 she was rammed by the Belgian liner *Vanderland*, 15 miles south-west of Portland. Severely damaged, she was towed all the way into Portland Harbour where she was repaired. The picture is particularly interesting. The *Angela* is a two-masted schooner of a type that had been trading around the coast of Europe for centuries. Here she is moored amongst Royal Navy warships of the Channel Fleet.

County of Anglesea

One of the luckiest ships ever to enter Weymouth Bay. The *County of Anglesea* struck on the Shambles Bank, south-east of Portland on the morning of 26 February 1905. As the tide fell her ballast shifted and she developed a heavy list. The crew , quite understandably, wanted to be taken off, and one jumped down into the lifeboat. The second man who tried to reach the lifeboat fell into the water between the vessels, and was only rescued with difficulty. The master of the *County of Anglesea* then forbade any more men to try and get off the ship, so they stayed on the ship as she was towed, still listing, into Weymouth Bay where she was righted.

Antwerp City

A few years later, in 1908, the *Antwerp City* proved that similar accidents could happen to steamships. Her cargo of grain had shifted after she had been struck by a heavy sea on 9 March. Amazingly her crew managed to keep her afloat and, canted over at an acute angle, she managed to steam into Portland Harbour three days later. As with the *County of Anglesea* she was righted and sailed again a few days later.

Kythnos

A fire on board ship is has always been a sailor's nightmare. In wooden vessels it was terrible; even in iron and steel vessels the idea of being trapped on a burning ship with nowhere to escape is, understandably, one of the worst fates a sailor can imagine.

The Greek vessel *Kythnos* caught fire in Portland Harbour, she was lucky, no one was seriously hurt, the fire was extinguished and the vessel saved.

Sandal

The *Sandal* very nearly became a major disaster, on 19 March 1903. She was a few miles east of Weymouth when a fire broke out in her engine room. This then spread to her cargo of esparto grass. The fire in her engine room was soon brought under control, however it proved impossible to put out the fire in her hold, so she was towed, still on fire, into Portland Harbour. Here trained firemen finally managed to extinguish the blaze. Remarkably she suffered little serious damage and was quickly repaired. Only nine days after the fire she was able to sail again under her own power.

Reliance

In 1949 the ketch *Reliance* ran into Cave Hole on Portland. Ann Davison, one of the two people on board described the wreck:

> Then the tall cliff face was upon us with a tremendous splintering crash. The bowsprit snapped like kindling. The flare was out. The night was dark. We clung to the mainsheets in a pool of light thrown by the lamps in front of the wheelhouse. She began to roll from side to side, rails under, with incredible speed, as if she would roll right over. A colossal jolt; the shock travelling from stem to stern. The mainmast sagged, came over, seemed to hang suspended. The boom dropped and we leapt from under. Before our horrified eyes the bows of the vessel buried into the very face of the cliff.'

(Ann Davison, Last Voyage.)

She survived though her husband was drowned.

Right: Reliance *stuck in Cave Hole. The woman on board is thought to be Ann Davison, the only survivor of the wreck.*

Below: Reliance *from Cave Hole.*

Lendor

On 8 September 1951 the yacht *Lendor* was sailing off Portland when her propeller caught in a lobster pot line. Helpless she drifted onto a ledge under Portland Bill. Despite desperate attempts to rescue her, remarkably captured on film, she sank in deep water just off the shore.

Opposite: *Trying to rescue the* Lendor.

Peregrine

Although she was wrecked in 1917, the *Peregrine* was not a casualty of war. Rather poor weather and errors in navigation led to her running onto the rocks at Portland Bill on 14 June. She was towed off the rocks the following month leaking badly. Despite this she was successfully towed into Portland Harbour where she received temporary repairs before continuing with her voyage.

Jolly Esmond

The delightfully named, *Jolly Esmond* went aground at Portland Bill on the evening of 26 August 1929. After a night of hard work, she managed to get off on the morning high tide under her own power.

Bournemouth

The wreck of the *Bournemouth* could have easily become a major disaster. On the afternoon of 27 August 1886 the paddle steamer *Bournemouth* left Torquay with over 200 excursion passengers on board; a second excursion steamer, the *Empress*, left at about the same time. It was never proved but many people suspected that the two vessels were racing back to Bournemouth. Fog descended, but the *Bournemouth* continued at high speed. About 7 pm, still travelling at 16 knots, she ran straight into the western coast of Portland. The weather, fortunately, was very calm and all the passengers were eventually taken off the vessel. Had the weather been bad, the outcome could have been very different as the *Bournemouth* was only carrying lifeboats for 45.

The *Bournemouth* broke her back on impact, and just rotted on the beach. Her remains can still be seen at low tide.

Ehen

Wrecks can happen in calm conditions too. On 21 April 1890 the French Barque *Ehen* drifted onto the rocks off Portland Bill. Holed, and taking on water, the crew of ten, and the single passenger, took to the ship's boats and fortunately managed to make their way to the shore safely. The *Ehen* drifted off the rocks and floated into Mutton Cove where her cargo of rice and pickles was successfully salvaged. The wreck later broke up.

Myrtledene

The *Myrtledene* was an elegant 2500-ton ore carrier, bound from Sagunto (Spain) to Rotterdam. On 25 March 1912 she ran aground at Mutton Cove on Portland. Her bottom had been badly damaged and her lower hull rapidly filled with water. The coastguards got a line on board and rescued her crew of 24 and two passengers. Despite her apparently undamaged state, there was no hope of saving her and she slid into deeper water. Divers know the wreck today for the wealth of marine life that can be found on it.

Opposite: *The Myrtledene aground.*

Turenne

The *Turenne* was a French trawler which was wrecked at Clay Hope on Portland on 12 February 1913. Her cargo of fish was quickly salvaged, but the vessel proved to be more difficult. Inspection showed that she had four holes in her hull and she was thought to be a total wreck.

A Portland quarry owner, Mr F. J. Barnes, had other ideas and bought the wreck for very little. He managed to get patches over the holes, drag her off and tow her round to Castletown Pier in Portland Harbour. Here she was finally broken up, making Mr Barnes a considerable profit.

Opposite: *Coming to see the shipwreck, the* Turenne *with schoolboys.*

Jason

On the morning of 13 March 1911 the small steamship *Jason* ran onto rocks off Portland. The Weymouth lifeboat *Friern Watch* stood by as three steam tugs managed to get lines on board and eventually towed her off.

Opposite: *The* Jason *being towed off with the lifeboat standing by.*

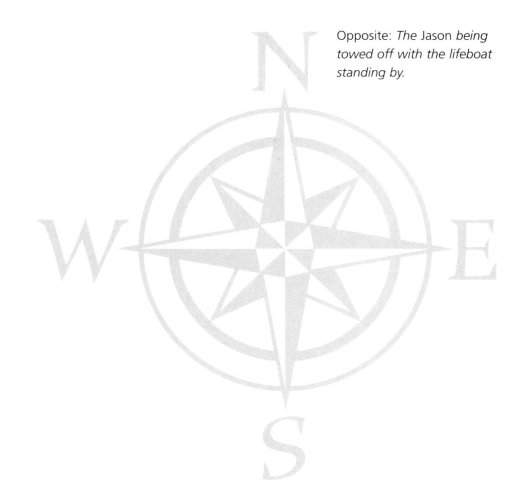

Minerve

The *Minerve* was a remarkable vessel. A French submarine which served throughout the Second World War, in 1940 her captain had refused to surrender at the fall of France, and instead sailed into Plymouth and handed the *Minerve* over to the British. After a few weeks the *Minerve* became one of the first ships in the Free French Navy, the Cross of Lorraine seen clearly on her conning tower. She was a small submarine, so was well suited to her wartime role of running missions along the Norwegian coast, slipping in and out of fjords, dropping off agents and supplies to partisans. Towards the end of the war an American aircraft attacked her, not recognising her unusual design. No one was hurt but her days of active service were over. She was used for training until 1945 when she was sent for breaking up. Under tow to the breakers yard the cable parted and she ran onto the western side of Portland. Salvage proved impossible, and she slipped into deeper water, where she still lies.

Right: Note the Cross of Lorraine, the symbol of the Free French Forces on her conning tower.

Gertrude

The steamship *Gertrude* was another casualty of fog. Poor visibility and bad navigation led to her running ashore at Blacknor Point on Portland on 26 August 1894. In the calm weather it was simple for the coastguard to rescue the crew of 18 and two passengers. However it proved impossible to salvage the vessel and she slipped down a boulder slope into deeper water. The wreck still lies there, her bow still pointing towards the shore. The surrounding seabed is littered with pieces of iron pyrites, the remains of her cargo.

Verbena

The *Verbena* was on her way from Saundersfoot in Pembrokshire to Weymouth with a cargo of culm (finely ground coal), when she was driven ashore at Blacknor Point on Portland on 22 July 1903. It proved to be impossible to get the vessel of the rocks, so she was sold where she lay, and broken up on the rocks.

Patroclus

The Blue Funnel liner *Patroclus* was homeward bound from Brisbane on 13 September 1907 when she ran onto Blacknor Point on Portland in dense fog. There were no passengers on board and, in the calm weather, there were no difficulties in rescuing the crew by breeches buoy, but saving the ship was more difficult. Initial inspection showed 14 feet of water in the forward hold. Despite this, with 11 steam pumps working on the deck, and five tugs pulling, she was dragged off the rocks and later repaired successfully.

The coastguard with the breeches buoy, as it was erected to rescue the crew.

Right: *Off-loading the cargo of the* Patroclus.

Below: *The* Patroclus *under repair in Portland Harbour.*

Okahandja

Fog was also the cause of the wreck of the German steamship *Okahandja*. On 8 June 1910 she was bound from Cartagena (Spain) to Stettin (now Szczecin, Poland) when she lost her way in dense fog and ran onto Tar Rocks on Portland, just to the north of Blacknor Point. The captain's wife and children were sent ashore by boat whilst the lifeboat stood by. The rocket apparatus was erected in case the crew needed to be evacuated, but the men worked hard and managed to get the pumps working and so saved their ship. Badly holed she was towed off by a salvage vessel and taken into Weymouth Harbour where she was given temporary repairs before sailing back to Germany.

Left: *The coastguard crew and the rocket apparatus, which was erected but never used.*

Below: *Sightseers coming to watch the salvage operation. One of the women in the boats is possibly the captain's wife.*

Opposite: *The Okahandja with salvage vessels in attendance.*

Bulow

The *Bulow* was a German liner on her way from Yokohama to Southampton when she ran aground near Blacknor Point on 18 June 1914. Although the weather was calm there was clearly concern for the safety of the passengers. All of them, nearly 300 were taken off to complete their journey by train. Tugs successfully got the *Bulow* off a few days later with no damage, so she too could continue to Southampton.

Winchester Castle

The *Winchester Castle,* a liner owned by the Union Castle Line, with 300 passengers on board, made a brief and unexpected visit to Portland on the night of 16 February 1936. Homeward-bound from Durban to Southampton, she was slightly off course and, in poor visibility, she grounded near Blacknor Point.

The Weymouth lifeboat stood by until it became clear that the ship was in no danger. As the tide rose she floated off and continued on to Southampton, her passengers none the worse for their adventure.

James Fennell

On 16 January 1920 the *James Fennell*, an Admiralty trawler bound from Gibraltar to Portsmouth ran onto rocks below Blacknor Point on Portland. What followed was one of the most remarkable rescues ever recorded on the Dorset Coast.

A Portland fisherman, Albert 'Sunny' Saunders heard a ship's siren from below Blacknor Point and suspected that a ship might be in trouble. Unable to see it because of the fog, he scrambled down the rocks and along the rocky shore. Seeing the *James Fennel* on the rocks he tried to get close, but failed because of the rising tide. So he climbed the cliffs and descended on the opposite side of the wreck. Wading waist deep he got close enough to catch a rope thrown from the ship. He tied it to a rock and helped the fifteen crew members onto shore. The captain was the last to leave, and slipped from the rope into the sea, but was rescued by Sunny and the crew.

Shortly afterwards salvage tugs tried to tow the *James Fennel* off the rocks, but as they did so she slid into deeper water, where she still lies.

Opposite: *'Sunny' Saunders and the rescued crew of the* James Fennel *.*

Preveza

Just one day before the *James Fennel* was wrecked, the *Preveza* had suffered a similar fate. She had been very unlucky. A Greek vessel, her owners were in financial trouble and this, almost certainly, lead to the loss of the vessel. She took on stores in Portland and then sailed for Cardiff. Here she had hoped to take on cargo, but the cargo owners refused to load their goods as the *Preveza* was uninsured. Returning to Portland she was enveloped in dense fog and, her crew not knowing where they were, ran her into Chesil Cove. There were various attempts to get her off, but these all failed and she was broken up on the beach, the salvage going to pay the local tradesmen who had not been paid for the stores she had taken on in Portland. The boilers remained on the beach and were local landmarks for many years. Their remains still lie underneath the shingle.

Opposite: *The* Preveza *from the top of Portland.*

The Preveza *with the salvage tug* Ellida. *At this time it was still hoped to get her off.*

Left: *The* Preveza *beginning to break up, – the schoolboys seem to be posing for the photographer.*

Opposite: *The end of the* Preveza.

Ellida

The *Ellida* was a salvage tug which tried to get the *Preveza* off Chesil Beach, but was very nearly wrecked herself. As she manoeuvred close inshore she put out an anchor in order to help her pull off if necessary, unfortunately the anchor cable snapped and wrapped round her propeller fixing her firmly to the beach. A second rescue attempt was now launched, to save the *Ellida*. After two days of hard work the cable finally parted and the *Ellida* was saved.

Opposite: *The* Ellida *on the beach with the wreck of the* Preveza *in the background.*

Madeleine Tristan

The *Madeleine Tristan* was a large three-masted schooner, which had once fished the Grand Banks off Newfoundland. On 19 September 1930 she was on a coasting voyage to Le Havre when she was driven into Chesil Cove, only a short distance from the remains of the *Preveza*. She was eventually thrown up high on the beach where she lay for many years as a prominent landmark, and playground for local children. Eventually she was declared a health hazard, as she had become infested with rats, and was cut up for firewood. A sad end for what was clearly a very beautiful ship.

Opposite: *The wreck of the* Madeleine Tristan *as a major tourist attraction.*

Coming to see the wreck of the Madeleine Tristan *was a popular family day out.*

The wreck of the Madeleine Tristan *with the* Preveza's *boilers in the foreground.*

MFV 1089

On Thursday 26 February 1953 the Royal Navy *MFV (Motor Fishing Vessel) 1089* developed engine trouble in thick fog off Chesil Beach. She ran aground, her crew not knowing where they were. Two of her crew swam for help, were very lucky and managed to reach the shore. They then walked, in freezing conditions, along the shingle for several miles until they were able to attract the attention of someone on the other side of the Fleet Lagoon.

The local coastguard reached the site of the wreck soon afterwards and managed to get a line on board, with which they took off the remaining crew. Two days later, when the weather had moderated, the destroyer HMS *Brocklesby* assisted in towing *MFV 1089* off the beach.

Nor

On 18 January 1887 the Norwegian steamship *Nor*, carrying salt from Cadiz to Bergen ran onto Chesil Beach, opposite Ferrybridge, in dense fog. The captain sounded the steam whistle continuously until the coastguard were alerted, they managed to get a line on board using the rocket apparatus and rescued all the crew.

The following day the wind got up, and began to bump the *Nor* on the bank on which she had grounded. By the end of the day she had begun to break up and slipped off the beach into deeper water. The remains still lie just off shore and are a popular dive site, her propeller standing vertically up from the sea bed.

Vera

On 8 March 1889 the *Vera*, bound from the Mediterranean to Hull ran onto Chesil Beach opposite Langton Herring. As well as her 28 passengers and crew, the coastguard also rescued three stowaways. Shortly after she had struck, the *Vera* slipped off the beach into deeper water where she still lies.

Emma Maria

The *Emma Maria*, a Russian schooner, was bound for Lisbon with a cargo of china clay. On the afternoon of 25 October 1903 she was seen to be in trouble in gale force winds in Lyme Bay. The steam tug *Petrel* got a line on board, but it parted after two hours of towing. Then the *Petrel* was damaged and had to return, leaving the *Emma Maria* anchored off Blacknor Point. After several hours of pitching and rolling the schooner broke free from her anchors and drove ashore on Chesil Beach. As she struck her mainmast fell over the side and formed a bridge to the shore. Without waiting to save anything the crew clambered along the mast to safety.

The following day a curious crowd gathered to 'see the wreck'. As the crowds gathered the *Patria* was driven onto the beach at the same spot. The crowd of sightseers quickly turned to rescuers.

Patria

As a young seaman, A.H. Rasmussen was on board the Norwegian barque *Patria* as she was being driven towards Chesil Beach on 26 October 1903. In his autobiography *Sea Fever*, he described the wreck:

The skipper called us aft.

'Boys,' he said, 'we have the choice between Chesil Bank and the cliffs of Portland. I think there is a chance of saving some of you if I attempt to sail her up on the beach instead of drifting in. Any objections?'

Chips spoke up for all of us: 'No sir, sail her up. It's the only way.'

'Square away fore and mainyards!' came the order 'Up helm!'

We jumped to it with a curious feeling of relief. The tension and weary waiting was over and we were facing a straight issue. 'Shake out the reef in the main upper topsail' came the next order and we youngsters swarmed up to cast off the reef points. 'Sea boots off and every man for himself!'

I was flung headlong over the side into the sea. In a few minutes I was caught up in a raging maelstrom of thundering seas. I could see the people on the beach quite clearly now, running down to help me out. I only remember dimly that I saw a man running towards me through that deadly surf with a rope around his waist. The next moment a great cheer from the beach as he grabbed me, and dozens of willing hands hauled us in.

'Her designer must have realised that she would probably be the last sailing-ship he would build, and he had lavished all his love and skill on her, so that the new generation of steamship men could see what a thing of speed and beauty a sailing-ship could be.'

(Rasmussen, *Sea Fever.*)

Right: *The* Patria *with the
remains of the* Emma Maria
in the foreground.

Below *The* Patria *broke
up, and together with her
cargo of wood, was
scattered in Chesil Cove.*

Lanoma

All that remained of the barque *Lanoma*, homeward-bound from Tasmania. On 8 March 1888 she was driven onto Chesil Beach opposite the village of Fleet. In the wreck 12 of her 18 crew were drowned and the vessel was smashed to pieces.

Dorothea

The Dutch vessel *Dorothea,* was driven ashore on Chesil Beach on the night of 14 February 1914. The crew all survived and were cared for by a local farmer who can be seen posing in front of the wreck. She lay on top of the beach for eight months, during which time she was sold twice, before being refloated in October. The salvage operation was very complex. First, the cargo of iron ore was off loaded, then the *Lyon*, a salvage vessel, tried to tow her off but she was too firmly embedded in the shingle. After this failure a different approach was tried, a wooden launching ramp was built and the *Dorothea* was launched sideways back into Lyme Bay, the *Lyon* pulling her down that ramp. The following year the *Dorothea* struck a mine in the North Sea and sank, again without loss of life.

Eighty years after her stranding, a geologist studying the pebbles on Chesil Beach found pieces of magnetite, a very rich iron ore. There was no way this could have reached the beach naturally, and from its location, was almost certainly part of the cargo of the *Dorothea*.

A family group pose beside the Dorothea. This may be one of the local families which assisted the crew after the wreck. One local farmer still possesses a decanter which was given to his grandfather by the captain of the Dorothea as a 'thank you' for his help.

The Dorothea *from the Abbotsbury Swannery. A fashionably dressed motoring party has stopped to look at the shipwreck.*

The Dorothea *and the salvage vessel* Lyon.

Bassurelle

On 15 July 1963 the French fishing boat *Bassurelle* was driven onto Chesil Beach, opposite Langton Herring, in a severe gale. Her engines having broken down she was swept ashore as so many vessels had been in the past. The bow of the vessel jammed onto the beach long enough for the crew to scramble ashore. Local boatmen then ferried them to safety across the Fleet, though there was some confusion as none of the rescuers spoke French and none of the crew knew any English.

The crew were very lucky as the *Bassurelle* broke up shortly afterwards leaving nothing that could be salvaged.

Lancelot

The *Lancelot* was a spritsail barge which ran ashore in bad weather on 27 November 1909, just to the west of the harbour piers at West Bay. Her rigging was much damaged, but she was otherwise intact. At the next spring tide she was towed of the beach and round into West Bay Harbour where she was repaired.

Alioth

Donald Payne in his 1953 book *Dorset Harbours* tells the sad tale of the *Alioth*:

On 3 May 1923, the iron-built sailing vessel *Alioth*, on passage from Gothenburg, arrived at Bridport to discharge her cargo of timber. She was the first German vessel to enter the harbour since the end of the Great War. By 10 May she had discharged her timber and loaded with sand and her captain was impatient to cast off. But there was a steady wind from the south, against which he could not beat out of harbour. Now there was at Bridport a motor-boat which would, for ten shillings [50p], tow a vessel far enough into Lyme Bay for her to tack past Portland. But the German skipper refused to pay ten shillings, and against all local advice, ordered the *Alioth* to be hobbled out – that is pushed to sea with boat-hooks. She cleared the harbour mouth, but before sail could be set, drifted helplessly ashore, less than a hundred yards from the eastern pier. It was her last voyage. A week later, in a westerly gale, she started to break up. It was a sad ending for the ship.

Index of vessels mentioned in the text

Further reading

Attwooll, M., 1998, *Shipwrecks* (Discover Dorset Series).

Davison, A., 1953, *Last Voyage*.

Farr, G., 1971, *Wreck and Rescue on the Dorset Coast*.

Francklyn, T., 1756, *Serious advice and fair warning to all that live upon the seacoast of England and Wales, particularly to those in the neighbourhood of Weymouth and Portland, addressed to them in a sermon*.

Hinchcliffe, J. & V., 1999, *Dive Dorset*.

Larn, R. & Larn, B., 1995, *Shipwreck Index of the British Isles, Volume 1: The South West*.

Mc Cartney, I., 2003, *Lost Patrols, Submarine Wrecks of the English Channel*.

Meade Faulkner, J., 1898, *Moonfleet*.

Payne, D., 1953, *Dorset Harbours*.

Pridham, L., 1956, *The Dorset Coastline*.

Rasmussen, A.H., 1952, *Sea Fever*.

Smith, C., 1796, *Narrative of the Loss of* The Catharine, Venus, *and* Piedmont *Transports and the* Thomas, Golden Grove, *and* Aeolus *Merchant Ships, near Weymouth, on Wednesday the 18th of November last drawn up from Information taken on the spot, and Published for the Benefit of an unfortunate Survivor from one of the wrecks and her infant Child*.

Smith, G., 1995, *Hampshire & Dorset Shipwrecks*.

Treves, Sir Frederick, 1906, *Highways and Byways in Dorset*.